VIETNAM NOW

John R Jones

Aston Publications

The Guardian of the Namh Dinh Temple.

Acknowledgements

Researching, photographing and writing a book of this sort requires the help of a lot of people.
For reasons of space they cannot all be mentioned by name. During many months in the country
I received help from no fewer than twenty-eight interpreters or guides from the tourist authorities in
many provinces. Special thanks, however, must go to my two great friends from Vietnam Tourism:
Lan Hinh, from Ho Chi Minh City, and Nguyen Duy Hoai, from Hanoi. The fact that I arrived back
in one piece is largely due to the efforts of my drivers, Cuong, Minh and Hoang, who transported me
15,000 km over the length and breadth of Vietnam.

My particular thanks to the following people, who allowed me access to their facilities and
provided me with much valuable information: Vo Si Thua, Director of the Nghia Binh Classical
Opera, for a special performance of the Tuong; Professor Nguyen Tan Thu, of the Hanoi
Acupuncture Institute; Kim Cuong, for access to a dental clinic in Hanoi; Le Van Loc, Director of the
Union of Mulberry Silk Companies in Da Nang; Le Xuan Ba, Director of the Dong Nai Ceramics
factory, and Ding Ngoc, of the Lacquerware factory in Ho Chi Minh City; Du Soh Mang and Hai
Hong, of the Ngha May shrimp factory; Nguyen Van Hinh of the Hau Giang pineapple processing
factory; Truong Phu Kien, who showed me round the shipbuilding works at Rach Gia; Trinh Chi, of
the Social Science Institution, for information on minority groups; Tran Sanh, Chief Monk at the
Khmer temple at Soc Trang.

I am indebted also to the following groups for their encouragement and assistance in my
researches: the staff of the publications *Vietnamese Studies, Vietnam and Vietnam Courier;* the staff of the
Vietnamese Embassy in London, for their help in obtaining visas; the authorities in the North, for
my visits to the Yen So co-operative, the Young Pioneer Club, the Martial Arts Festival and a variety
of schools in the Hanoi area; the authorities in the South, for organizing visits to a number of
factories in the Mekong Delta, and for their help in the negotiations involved in obtaining
permission to photograph the minorities around Buon Ma Thuot, the Cao Dai Temple at Tay Ninh
and the Ossuary at Ba Chuc.

Finally, a very special thanks to the people of Vietnam, for the warmth of the welcome
I received wherever I went. They went through thirty years of almost continual warfare, during
which their country was virtually destroyed. As you will see from the photographs in this book,
they came out smiling.

This book is dedicated to the memory of my mother.

Map of Vietnam

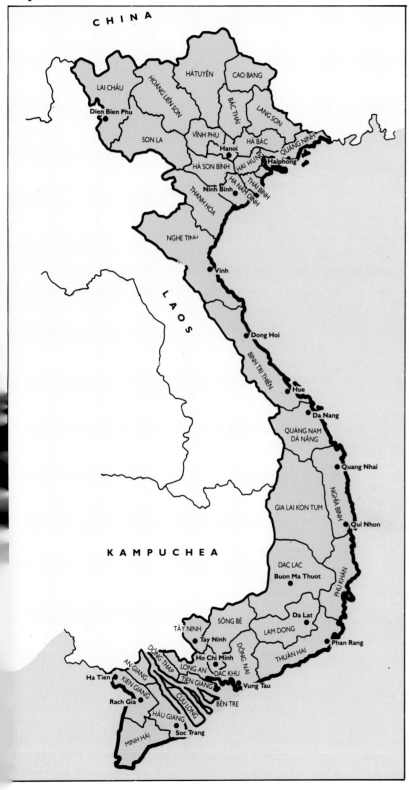

Contents

Introduction

The name Vietnam, 'Beyond the South', was probably more applicable when its southern border at the Ngang Pass divided it from the 'Kingdom of Champa'. Now occupying approximately one-half of the total area of Indo-China, it holds a very important geographical position in South East Asia. Throughout its history, conflicts have raged upon its borders and within its very heart. Few countries have experience of such devastating human suffering at the hand of foreign aggressors, the Chinese, Mongols, Siamese, French, Japanese, Kampucheans and recently the conflict known to the world as the 'Vietnam War'.

This book is not about war. It is about the land, its cities, towns and villages, and what they are like now. It is about the children, who have not experienced the ravages of war. It is about their parents, their past, their everyday lives and their aspirations for the future.

Readers have an opportunity to see the smiling faces of courageous, friendly, sensitive, tenacious people who are rebuilding their country in every way that is possible.

The enormous amounts of publicity the country has received has stirred people's imaginations world-wide. Thousands of tourists are visiting every year; *Vietnam Now* is an insight into what they will experience.

(*Left*) This Buddhist school is in the citadel of Co Loa, in Dong Anh district. The temple is dedicated to King An Duong, and narrowly escaped a direct hit during the bombing raids on the North in 1972.

(*Right*) A Schoolboy at the Truc Trung Primary School reads aloud a section of Kim Van Kieu. It is a poetic account of the love of Kim Trong, who praises his sweetheart Thuy Kieu, the Princess of the Moon. This book greatly influences the lives of Vietnamese schoolchildren. They are encouraged to learn it thoroughly, and many can quote large sections of it.

(*Left*) A little girl takes flowers for her teacher on National Teachers' Day – 20 November.

(*Below*) One way of keeping cool.

(*Right*) Children in Xuan Loc district – Dong Nai province.

History

Archaeological studies have suggested that the ancient Vietnamese people existed 300,000-500,000 years ago in the swampy woods of the Red River delta. According to ancient legends and folklore, King Loc Tuc (2879 BC) married the daughter of the God of the Seas. Their son Lac Long Quan and his wife Au Co had 100 sons. One of them, their eldest, ruled the ancient Kingdom of Van Lang.

Vietnam has faced countless struggles against aggressors from this period of the Hung kings right through to the present century. The Han Chinese ruled the country for 1,000 years from 111 BC, during which the efforts of the Trung sisters (AD 40-43), Trieu Thi (248) and Mai Thuc Loan (722) failed to gain permanent independence. It was Ngo Quyen, in 944, who put an end to 1,000 years of Chinese feudal dominance.

At the time when King Dinh Bo Linh came to the throne (968) the armies of Champa were attacking deep into Vietnamese territory from the south. King Dinh, together with his successor General Le (980), overthrew the Chinese and Cham invaders.

The new line of rulers that followed, the Buddhist Ly King, Ly Thuong Kiet and Tran Hung Dao, the most powerful of the 12 Tran kings, overthrew the Chinese and defeated the mighty armies of Kublai Khan.

During the Ho Dynasty (1400-1407), China once more gained the upper hand, but this was only to be short-lived. The national hero, King Le Thai To, known as Le Loi, the Great Administrator, defeated the Minh in 1418.

The second Le Dynasty, 1428-1527, saw the nine kings gaining further ground from the kingdom of Champa. The border of Vietnam then extended deep into the present-day central provinces.

King Dinh Bo Linh, in the Nam Dinh Temple at Hoa Lu.

The famous Tay Son rebellion, led by Nguyen Hue, occurred during the 3rd Le Dynasty (1533-1788). This ended the exploitation of the peasants by the Trinh and Nguyen lords. The regime ended when Nguyen Anh proclaimed himself Emperor Gia Long in 1802 in the ancient Imperial capital Hue. By the beginning of the rule of the 13 Nguyen kings, Champa had been totally overthrown and the coastline of Vietnam now extended for well over 2,000 km.

During the period of French rule, which began in 1858, Vietnam became divided into Tonkin in the north, Annam in the centre, and Cochinchina in the south and the struggle for liberation became intense during the 1883-1945 period. The people's resistance movements increased and many new political parties came into being. None were more powerful than the Viet-Nam-Doc-Lap-Dong-Minh-Hoi, known as the Viet-Minh, led by Ho Chi Minh. This League for the Independence of Vietnam was formed in 1940, one year before the Japanese invaded.

In August 1945 the 'Democratic Republic of Vietnam' was formed under Ho Chi Minh's leadership, but independence was only short lived. The French regained control in 1947 and held it until 1954, when they were beaten during the battle of Dien Bien Phu.

General Le Hoan (*left*), who succeeded Dinh Bo Linh and also inherited his wife, Duong Van Nga (*right*).

The shrine dedicated to Quang Trung, leader of the
Tay Son rebellion.

The first major Indochina war was over, but the series of events during which American aid was given to the South escalated into the horrific 'Vietnam War', known to the Vietnamese as the 'American War'. Bombing raids deep into North Vietnam had started before the troop arrivals at Danang on 8 March 1965; they were to continue right through to 1973. By then 7 million tons of bombs, including phosphorus, napalm and thousands of gallons of chemical defoliants, had been dropped, and 25 million bomb craters poxed the landscape.

Despite the American involvement the North Vietnamese armies had advanced across the 17th parallel in 1972 and by March 1975 they had overthrown Buon Ma Thuot and Hue. The final blow came when the NLF tanks appeared on Le Duan Boulevard in Saigon before crashing through the gates of the headquarters of the South Vietnamese government.

Even after the end of the second Indochina war the country has not been totally peaceful. There have been invasions from Kampuchea on to Vietnam's border provinces in the Mekong Delta. Thousands were killed by Pol Pot's troops between 1977 and 1978, and there is always a threat from China. But despite all, the Vietnamese people remain steadfast and undaunted.

The remains of a Russian T54 tank on the road between Quang Tri and Hue.

The Northern Provinces

The first glimpse of the northern provinces of Vietnam is often from an ancient Ilyushin 18 turbo-prop of the national airline. As it descends over the bomb-cratered paddy fields towards the plain of Bac Bo, Mount Ba Vi stands proud like a statue overlooking the Red River granaries. To the east, beyond Hongai, are the magnificent seascapes of Halong Bay with thousands of small islets scattered over emerald green waters. To the north and west, jagged karstic mammillate promontories stretch all the way to the mountains of Viet Bac and the border with Laos.

The Northerners are tough resilient people who have weathered many storms. In the past they have included the female general Trieu Thi Trinh, who, in Thanh Hoa province in AD 248, fought off the Chinese. Well remembered are King Dinh and General Le (10th century), and Le Thai To and Le Loi (15th century), who gained resounding victories against the Ming. The northern provinces are the homes of wiry mountain tribes, many of which live in the inaccessible border provinces adjoining China.

Karst mountain area near Hoa Binh.

The people, often born into bloodshed and turmoil, still remember how American bombers virtually razed the Kham Thien and An Duong districts in Hanoi. Cemented in their minds are the cruel struggles against the French, culminating in the battle of Dien Bien Phu, and the Declaration of Independence read by President Ho Chi Minh. As they go about their everyday business in a city of lakes, pagodas and French villas, the roads teeming with bicycles, their broad grins hide the scars which remain in their hearts. They look forward to their festivals – Tet, a time of rebirth, meditation and hope, and the Huong Tich pilgrimage to the sacred mountain.

Peace has returned to this land and the people carry on their everyday tasks of planting and threshing rice, herding ducks, selling produce, producing lime and responding to any challenges and difficulties. Not even the centuries of war against the Chinese can destroy their culture. Daily visits are paid to pagodas with beautifully carved wood furnishings showing historic scenes, floral motifs, dragons, unicorns, tortoises and phoenixes.

Their morale has never been so high. The ancient mandarin route from the south is now free of obstacles, bridges have been rebuilt and the railway once more transports produce to the central provinces and beyond.

Muong woman (*above top*).

Tay woman, Son la (*above*).

(*Opposite*) Meo woman from Dien Bien Phu.

(*Left*) White Thai girl carrying a string of dragonflies. Around her neck is an American ID tag.

(*Opposite*) White Thai men panning for gold at Mai Chau.

(*Below*) A typical street scene in Hanoi.

Hanoi

Translated into English the word Hanoi means 'the city inside a bend of the Red River'. When it existed as a small village where the To Lich joined the Red River, it was called the 'Dragon's Navel'. For eight centuries until the beginning of the Ly Dynasty (1010), the capital of Vietnam was at Hoa Lu, now a favourite tourist spot near the town of Ninh Binh. It was King Ly Cong who established the capital, then known as Thang Long, on its present-day site. At this time a royal city was constructed, at the centre of which was the Forbidden City where the king lived with his concubines.

During the reign of the Ly kings, 1010–1225, the National Academy (Temple of Literature 1070) and the One Pillar Pagoda (1049) were constructed. The most active Buddhist Centre in Hanoi, the Quan Su Pagoda, and the Pagoda of the Stone Lady (Ba Da) followed in the 15th century.

In the centre of Hanoi 'the lake of the restored sword' remains as a reminder of the victory of Le Loi against Ming aggressors in the 15th century. Here, his sacred sword, Long Quan, was returned to the waters after it was taken by a golden turtle. The lake known as Ho Hoan Kiem is still famous for its huge turtles; one caught in 1968 weighed 250 kg! In the 18th century Hanoi was the site of the battle in which Tay Son King Nguyen Hue

(Quang Trung) defeated a 200,000 strong Manchu army. His victory is still celebrated at the Dong Da festival.

In 1802 the capital of Vietnam was moved to Hue. From 1882 to 1954 Hanoi was mostly under French rule. In April 1966 American bombers came and raids were to continue until 30 December 1972. Since then most of the razed areas have been rebuilt and it is reported that over 11 million new houses have appeared in the north.

Pilgrims travel from miles around to pray at the shrine of the One Pillar Pagoda (Chua Mot Cot). The statue inside is of Quan Am.

Driving in from Gia Lam airport many tourists still expect to see a devastated Hanoi. Instead there is hardly any indication of war destruction. Seas of conical hats transported by thousands of bicycles stream through the wide French boulevards, which echo with the names of famous generals, kings and battle areas, Nguyen Khoai, Hung Vuong and Dien Bien Phu. Old French trams trundle through streets named after insurrectionalists: Cao Thang, Ba Trieu and Cao Ba Quat.

In the old quarter is number 48 Hang Ngang Street, where Ho Chi Minh wrote the Declaration of Independence in 1945. It is easy to get lost amongst the mass of tiny streets with magical names such as Cotton Street, Broiled Fish Street, Brine Street, Sugar Street, Medicine Street. Interesting smells waft into the nostrils from the flower market on Hang Luoc Street and the small restaurants selling Pho (Vietnamese soup), Ech Tam Bot Ran (frog meat), Oc Nhoi (snail) and Gio (rolled up pork).

There is plenty to attract the thousands of tourists who visit Hanoi every year. In the evening the central theatre, Duong Trang Tien, has even put on a performance of Swan Lake, but more traditionally there is the Tuong (classical opera) or the Cheo (traditional theatre). There are dances, usually sixties style, in the Thang Loi and Thong Nhat hotels, Bao Chi (journalists' club) and the Australian Embassy's Billabong Club. During the day there are plenty of tourist sites — pagodas, lakes, co-operatives, craft centres and museums.

The Quan Su Pagoda (*above*) was built in the first Le dynasty as a Buddhist sanctuary for visitors from Laos, Cambodia and Champa.

(*Opposite*) The central shrine in the Quan Su Pagoda. Sakya Mouni is the Buddha of the Present, Dida is the Buddha of the Past, and Di Lac, once a philosopher, is the Buddha of the Future. Quan Am, or Thi Kinh, is a Boddisatra. They are all important figures in Vietnamese Buddhism.

The Chua Thay (Thay) Pagoda is 60 km from Hanoi in Sai Son village, Quoc Dai district. This Buddhist pagoda, built in the 11th century during the Ly Dynasty, contains two main pavilions housing important Buddhist statues.

The statue with the yellow robe is To Doa Hanh, the son of Tu Vinh. He was once a doctor in his native village and on his death was buried in a cave on the mountain next to the Thay Pagoda. There is a story which tells of King Ly Than Tong and his wife Sung Hien Hau in the 11th century. They visited the pagoda to pray for a son. To Doa Hanh was believed to have been reincarnated as their son.

(*Left*) A statue representing Sakya Mouni at birth, surrounded by nine dragons. The Ba Da Pagoda, which houses it, is the centre of the Hanoi Buddhist Association. It was damaged by the Chinese in the 15th century and razed by the French. The magnificent central altar was the only part of the original Pagoda which remained completely intact.

(*Right*) Visitors to the Thay Pagoda.

Opposite) The main altar of the Thay Pagoda.

(*Opposite*) The Temple of Literature is a peaceful
setting for artistic composition.

(*Right*) Weapons training.

The Quoc Tu Giam, known as the Temple of Literature or Van Mieu, was originally dedicated to the cult of Confucius. It was once the National Academy, where scholars of feudal Vietnam were educated. It was founded under the Ly Dynasty. Confucius, or Kong Qiu as he was known to scholars, was a nobleman from the Chinese Lu state who devoted his whole life to study.

The most prominent features of the temple are the 82 monolithic stelae on 82 stone tortoise pedestals, each dedicated to one of the triennial examinations of doctors of literature. The rest of the Temple is composed of many gates and pavilions and is still the site of artistic studies.

The original teachings of the Academy consisted of four classical works—the Dai Hoc (Great Study), the Trung Dung (Middle and unchanging course), Luan Ngu (Teachings of Confucius) and the Manh Tu (Mencius writings). Five important books based on science and arts subjects were used in the Academy.

During the Peasants' Revolt of the 18th century the Academy was barely used despite attempts at revival. During the reign of Gia Long, when the capital was transferred to Hue, a new National Academy was established there.

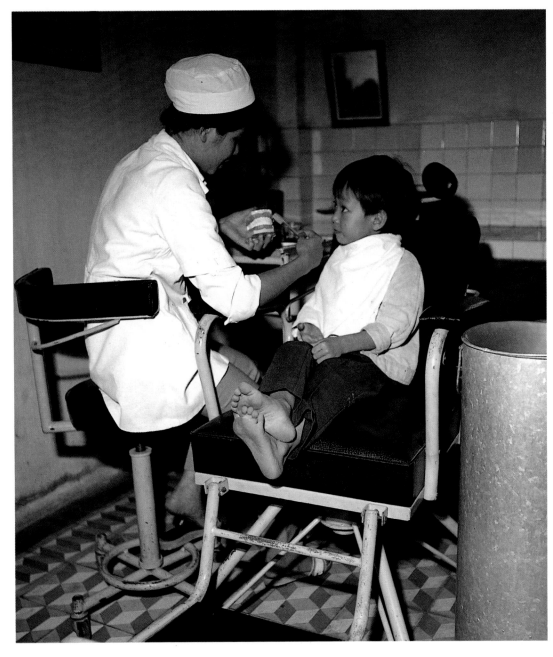

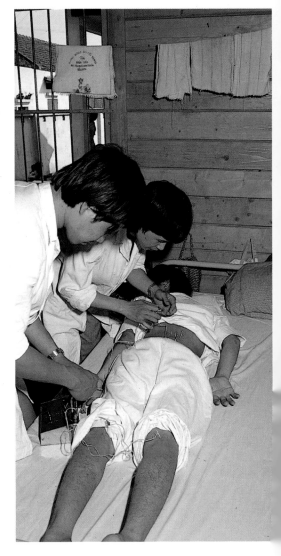

(*Above*) Students receiving instruction in techniques at the Acupuncture Institute. The patient is receiving treatment for backache.

(*Left*) Training in dentistry at the Trung Vuong School.

The Acupuncture Institute in Hanoi is the only one in the world to operate independently of a hospital. There are 60 doctors in residence and another 90 medical workers and attendants. Set up in 1982, the Institute is headed by Professor Nguyen Tau Thu, who is a recognized world authority on acupuncture.

A major breakthrough at the Institute has been the treatment of blindness due to meningitis. Most people in Hanoi know the story of the little girl, Ta Thi Thuy, who was found to be completely blind following an attack of meningitis. After only four sessions of electric acupuncture the child's sight was restored. Since then the Professor has been able to restore the sight of 23 children who had become blind through the disease. Patients are transferred to the Institute from Bach Mai hospital, now rebuilt after being destroyed by US bombers in December 1972.

(*Left*) Rope-seller in the old part of Hanoi, once known as Dong Kinh Nghia Thuc, after the movement set up here which led to the August 1945 revolution. The ropes sold here are made from coconut bristles at Tam Quan.

(*Below Left*) The wares of a medicinal herbseller, Medicine street. Of the 6,000 plants grown in Vietnam, more than one thousand are listed as medicinal. Plants sold include anti-bacterial types such as *Euphorbiaceae*, cinnamon and eucalyptus. An interesting plant is Lanterwin, which during the Vietnam War was used to heal wounds on the soft parts of the body. Soldiers sometimes carried Dinh Nam as a remedy for dysentery. Powder from the stone of the Longane tree is sold as a cure for blisters.

A funeral wreath maker in Hang Luoc street (*below*)

(*Left*) The Young Pioneer Club can accommodate 5,000 children, and there are smaller clubs in every district. These boys are training in Karate, only one of the forms of martial arts taught here.

(*Right*) Uncle Ho occupies a special place in the history of Vietnam. His statue dominates the scene at this Martial Arts Festival.

Vo Vietnam martial arts (*below*).

The Vietnamese people have devised and developed many methods of self-defence and combat, with and without arms. The Young Pioneer Club, opened in Hanoi in June 1955, has been keen to train youngsters to play an important role in national defence.

The youngsters in the northern provinces practise different types of martial arts. 'Vo Vietnam' has certain movements similar to those used by the Binh Dinh fighting school in the central provinces which allow smaller opponents to utilise their meagre strength to maximum advantage. In this way it has similarities to 'Tay Son Vo Si' used by Nguyen Hue to train his soliders during the Tay Son rebellion.

The club is keen that they also know karate; many begin when they are only three years old. They have received visits from masters of the Nhat Nam School in north central Vietnam. This school uses the traditional techniques of the ancient Hoan and Ai areas in Thanh Hoa province. Recently they were privileged to have a visit from the Grand Master of Lieu Doi School of Martial Arts in Ha Nam Ninh province.

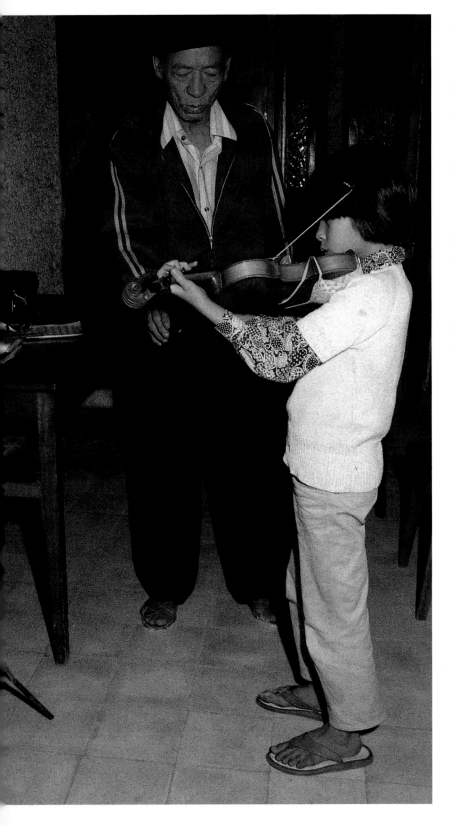

Two other aspects of the Young Pioneer Club. (*Above*) Young girls receiving ballet training. From here, many hope to continue at the Viet Bac Cultural and Art School at Thai Nguyen. (*Left*) A Master passes on some tips to a young violinist.

The main department stores on Trang Tien and Nam Bo are reminiscent of Chinese cities. The shelves are, however, barer and queues form quickly when new items are for sale. Luxury goods are available to the privileged in state shops, where the dollar is king. Books in English are very difficult to buy, but maps and posters are freely available. The souvenir shops stock rattan goods, basketry, porcelain, jewellery and lacquerware.

(*Above*) The interior of a Poster shop on Trang Tien Street.

(*Left*) Department store on Trang Tien street.

A reading room (*below*).

The circus in Hanoi.

The Tet Festival

Tet is believed to be of Chinese origin. Nowadays it shows only a remote resemblance to a Chinese festival. Tet is a calendar date, the first day of the lunar year, and occurs at the beginning of the spring equinox. This timing is of great significance for an agricultural nation such as Vietnam. It is a time when people should be friendly with everyone, and the Vietnamese believe that by ridding all his thoughts of evil, man contributes to the general concourse of the universe. During the three days, the deceased take part in the life of their descendants. On Tet eve they are invited, through a ceremony of sacrifice, to come back to the family and have their share of the general joy.

On the morning of New Year's first day, each family is concerned about who is going to be the first visitor because the latter may affect the fate of all the family members for the whole year. If the first visitor is a happy man, happiness is ensured until the next Tet, so the first visit is often contrived, among relatives and friends. The one who is considered the happiest is selected and asked to come as early as possible on that day. An ancient Tet custom is Cay Neu, the setting up of a bamboo pole in front of each house. A small basket on top of the pole contains betel and areca nuts. A small square of woven bamboo above the basket stops evil spirits. The Cay Neu shows the evil spirits that Buddha's protection is extended to the home. Another tradition is to scatter lime powder around the house which gives protection against evil spirits that will not be frightened off by the Cay Neu.

The apricot tree and the narcissus used to assume great importance during Tet, but now they have lost their old magical character and are used more as an adornment. Tet begins with the Giao Thua, which marks the transition from one year to another. During the previous afternoon a ceremony known as Ta Nien occurs in which a sacrifice is offered to the deceased. On the morning of the first day of Tet everyone gets up early, and dishes are prepared which will be the first offerings of the year to the ancestors. Wishes of happiness are exchanged with every person, friend or foe. Monetary gifts are passed on in red envelopes, red being the colour of luck. Flowers are favourite presents because they make a person's home more welcoming to good spirits. Firecrackers are let off in their thousands, and in many cities, towns and villages the Dragon Dance is performed. The

Tet is a time for wearing brand new clothes. If, on the morning of Tet, a child wears the previous day's clothes, it is considered a humiliating acknowledgement of poverty on the part of the family concerned.

Tet is a very profitable time for the firecracker sellers of Binh Da.

fourth day marks the end of Tet — this is the day the ancestors return to their heavenly abode. The Cay Neu is removed on the seventh day of the first month.

Tet would not be celebrated properly if the coming of the new year was not greeted by the crackling of countless firecrackers. The best are made in Binh Da, about 35 km from Hanoi. An explanation of why firecrackers are set off during Tet comes from the legend by Thien Nguyet Linh. It related to the wicked spirits called Na-Ong and his wife Na-Ba, both of whom fostered an obstinate hatred of mankind. They mainly played their nasty tricks at night, but were very afraid of light and noise. At Tet people used to light their houses and fired crackers to scare then away. Now the purpose of using firecrackers is to make as much noise as possible.

The Dragon Dance (shown above) has its origins in the 'Rong Ran' — the Dragon snake game played by children on moonlit nights, particularly on the full moons of the seventh and eighth months of the lunar year and the Tet festival. In this game, children form a single file with an adult in the lead to fight back any opponent who tries to snatch one member from the row.

Another theory links the Dragon Dance to the legend about the early ancestors of the Vietnamese people, according to which the union between the Dragon, who inhabited the mountain, and the fairy, who ruled the sea, gave birth to 100 eggs which later hatched into the various tribes who settled in the present territory of Vietnam.

There is also an unquestionable link between the Dragon Dance and other games such as the Unicorn or Lion dances, which remain very popular in the country. The dance requires the harmonious movements of all the dancers. The dragon undulates leisurely and then breaks into a vivacious movement, with all the performers swaying energetically under the belly of the mythical beast.

(*Opposite*) A religious procession moves through the village of Binh Minh.

The Le Te ceremony (*left*), dedicated to Lac Long Quan, takes place in the midday heat.

(*Below*) Band accompaniment for the Le Te ceremony.

The Lac Long Quan Festival

The Lac Long Quan Festival is held from the first to the sixth day of the third lunar month at Binh Minh village, Thanh Oai district, Ha Son Binh province. It is dedicated to Lac Long Quan, who is allegedly the ancestor of the Vietnamese. According to legend, his wife Au Co produced 100 eggs which became one hundred sons. Fifty of the sons followed their mother to the mountains and the rest settled in the Delta.

The festival begins with the Le Te, a ceremony which is dedicated to Lac Long Quan. During this the elders of Binh Minh, wearing traditional costume, pay homage in front of a colourfully decorated altar. Traditional music and dances are performed during the ceremony, whilst wine and flowers are presented at the main altar. A long procession then follows, when altars loaded with flowers and fruit are carried by young ladies through the street of Binh Minh village. There are other festivities, including firework displays and wrestling, which prove to be a big attraction to the villagers.

The start of a pilgrimage to the Pagoda of Perfume.

The Festival at the Pagoda of Perfume, Huong Tich

The Festival at the Pagoda of Perfume, Huong Tich, occurs in the spring in the Huong Son mountains, My Duc district, Ha Son Binh province. After 60 km of travel from Hanoi, visitors arrive at Huong Son commune. From here a boat transports pilgrims along small canals surrounded by limestone peaks, some of which are over 2 million years old (see the photograph on page 13). These mountains have names such as The Cock, The Nun and The Crouching Elephant.

It is a one-hour boat ride before the docking area for the long climb to Huong Tich is reached. Thousands of pilgrims, many barefoot, make their way up the tortuous stony paths, visitors greeting each other by saying 'A Di Da Phat' (may Buddha bless you). Although there are many refreshment areas *en route*, it is a tough climb.

The main Huong Tich grotto has a joss stick smoky atmosphere; the smell of incense is everywhere. A large banner at the entrance to the cave can barely be seen; stalactites and stalagmites gleam when the choking smoke disappears temporarily. The atmosphere is one of religious devotion.

The main grotto at Huong Tich.

Above) A brick kiln in Com Binh district, near Hai Duong.

Opposite) A lime kiln near Hai Phong.

It is reported that over 11 million new houses have been constructed in the north to replace those destroyed or damaged during the war. Lime kilns have sprung up everywhere to provide a cement base for the reconstruction programme, and there are many brick-making kilns throughout the fertile rice-growing region. Buffalo carts transport building materials to Hai Duong, the nearest rail stop.

A view of the fishing harbour at Halong Bay.

Halong Bay lies to the north-east of Hai Phong, and is reached by two ferry crossings. A good panoramic view of the bay is obtained by heading north-east for the town of Hongai. The panoramic view of Halong Bay can also be appreciated from a boat as it glides its way through rocky islets described by poets such as Nguyen Du as tortoise-shaped, looking like toads, dragons, fighting cocks and even men's heads. The rocks have wonderfully lyrical names such as Rua, Coc and Rong. On one island known locally as Khi, monkeys are used in experiments to develop a vaccine against poliomyelitis. A very famous limestone islet is 'Ciau Go'—the hiding place of the wooden stakes—named after a famous battle in which wooden stakes were used to trap a mongol fleet as it sailed down the Bach Dang River.

Many visitors come to the area to visit Hoa Lu, the capital of ancient Vietnam from 968 to 1010: Hoa Lu means Flower Gate. The locals still call it Reed Flowers because King Dinh Bo Linh, when he was a child, organized mock battles with his friends in which reed flowers were used as flags. He was important in defeating twelve regional feudal lords and bringing about the reunification of a divided country.

The statues of King Dinh and his three sons, Dinh Quoc Lien, Dinh Hang Lang and Dinh Toan, are inside the Dinh temple. The temple courtyard is reached by an outer triumphal gate — Nghi Mon Ngoai — and an inner triumphal gate — Nghi Mon Noi. Passing through the east-facing door one observes large old Vietnamese characters which, translated, say 'From this point on we have our independence'. Another temple just up the road is the Le temple, which contains the figures of General Le Hoan, who succeeded King Dinh and inherited his wife and children.

(*Above*) King Dinh Bo Linh in the Nam Dinh Temple at Hoa Lu, the ancient capital, which is near Ninh Binh in Ha Nam Ninh province.

(*Right*) Visitors to the Bich Dong Pagoda.

During the Den festival people come to see a game called 'fighting with the reed flags' popularized by King Dinh. They visit the magnificent scenery in the Truong Yen area—very popular are the caves known as the Bich Dong, which are surrounded by The Five Elements Mountain. Boats can be hired which will take the tourists along a little tributary of the Hoang Long River, and these can be rowed right under the mountain. It is an interesting way of getting to the Bich Dong Pagoda, arranged in three levels, from the top of which can be seen mountains bearing the names of birds: Phi Duyen, Flying Hawk; Hoi Hac, Returning Crane, and Duc Thuy, Bathing Kingfisher.

Work on the railway system between Hanoi and Saigon started in 1902, but due to the lack of finances and many political problems, the next phase of construction was not until the 1936-1941 period. During the war against the French, and later the Americans, virtually all the line became inoperable. By 1978 almost 1,300 km, together with most of the bridges, had been rebuilt. The most important bridge was undoubtedly that at Thanh Hoa, spanning the Song Ma River. Between 1965 and 1968 North Vietnamese forces heavily defended it from over 100 attacks by American aircraft. Finally, on 27 April 1972, it was destroyed by the new highly sophisticated laser-guided 'smart' bombs. The train pictured has just crossed the new Ham Rong bridge and is heading south to the central provinces.

The Central Provinces

Regions have always been known to the Vietnamese as Ky. The central region Trung Ky extends from Vinh, the capital of Nghe Tinh province, to Quy Nhon in Nghia Binh.

The people from this area have the reputation of being bold, dauntless, jocular, wiry individuals. They include President Ho Chi Minh, the Viet Minh commander Vo Nguyen Giap, the great scholar Nguyen Cong Tru and the poet Nguyen Du. It was he who wrote the immortal Kim Van Kieu, which every Vietnamese child knows by heart.

The central provinces now include most of the ancient Kingdom of Champa, which was taken from the Cham people by the Vietnamese in the 17th and 18th centuries. Vestiges of the ancient temples and lofty towers of the 'Amaravati' and 'Vijaya' Cham centres can be seen right through from the Truong Son mountains to Quy Nhon.

Riots have raged in the provinces throughout history, Tay Son against the Trinh and Nguyen lords, Nghe Tinh 'soviets', peasants who rose up against the French in Vinh, and Buddhists who demonstrated against the Diem regime at Hue.

Warfare through the centuries has taken its toll in human lives, suffering, and damage to priceless architectural structures, including the Imperial City of Hue. Chemical defoliants have prevented crops growing and in many areas, particularly the 17th parallel region, bomb craters are still being filled in.

Early morning rush hour in Vinh.

46

Natural disasters have spread like locusts; floods have hit Hue and Vinh and brought seawater into the rice fields in Binh Tri Thien. Sand erosion has lowered soil fertility from Can Loc to Cam Xuyen, around Dong Hoi and throughout Quang Nam Da Nang province. Typhoons have struck repeatedly.

Despite everything, the provinces have retained their natural beauty. Visitors marvel at the ruggedness of the Hoanh Son and Hai Van mountains. They comment on the majesty of the marble mountain, the tranquillity of the Perfume River and beauty of the virgin seascapes. They discover that the floods have been tamed by dykes, the sand barred by filao pines, and the land, at least in part, is fertile again. The rice fields on the plains of Quynh Luu, Dien Chau, Duy Xuyen and Phu Cat now shine a vivid green. The red basaltic soils of the highlands are rich in trees, coffee, tea, sesame, beans, cinchona and ginseng. The ancient Imperial capital of the Nguyen emperors is receiving a facelift, the Ben Hai river bridge is now open, and the sleepy ports of Danang and Quy Nhon are stirring.

(*Above*) Ho Chi Minh's native residence in the village of Chua, Nghe Tinh province.

(*Below*) A pipe-seller at Cho Vinh.

Nghe Tinh province

Nghe Tinh province, most of which lies in central Vietnam, bordered Champa in the 10th century. Before that, 4,000 years ago, it was inhabited by tribes of Van Lang. Throughout history it has always been a strategic position for military advancement against the northern provinces. Le Loi, Nguyen Trai and Nguyen Hue used it for this purpose. It became a massive battlefield when the Chinese attacked in the 7th century, the Mongols in the 12th century, the French particularly during the 1946-54 period, and the Americans between 1964 and 1968 and 1972-73.

The province, which extends from the 20th to the 18th parallel, includes the lands below the Chu River to the Transversal Pass through the Hoanh Son mountains. From the rice country of Quynh Luu the traveller can journey from the Tinh Gia chain of hills down towards the plain of Dien Chau. Towards the north-west, oranges and rubber flourish; beyond are the mountains of Laos.

Warm winds accompany the visitor, blowing in from the Truong Son range, which extends the whole length of the province. Dien Chau, which means 'land of underground water', has been extensively drained since the Vach Bac hydraulic system was completed in December 1976. Pineapples, rice and even tea flourish on land once waterlogged.

Logging camps have appeared in the dense forests north-west of Nghi Loc, from where huge lorries loaded with ironwood and ebony transport their logs to the railway station at Vinh.

To many, the capital Vinh marks the beginning of the central provinces of Vietnam. It has, during its history, suffered disaster after disaster. In 1952 the French bombed the province, and the 'scorched earth' policy saw Vinh burnt to the ground by its own inhabitants rather than surrender it to the French. Vinh was in ruins in 1954, but by 1964 it had been extensively rebuilt. Then it was hit by American bombers. The city, which is strategically positioned as a gateway to the south and west, was completely razed. The tough people of Vinh remember vividly the troublesome 1965-72 period, and the heavy bombing raids between April 1972 and January 1973.

The area has also suffered its fair share of natural disasters due to extensive flooding by the tributaries of the Ca River, the Ngan Pho, Gianh and Hieu.

South of Vinh the gateway to other central provinces extends through the Ngan Sau valley on to the infertile sandy plains of Can Loc. Through Thach Ha, Hatinh and Cam Xuyen huge sand banks line the roadsides. This is a no-man's-land where only Rhodomyrty grass will grow.

Still further south, beyond Kyanh, the Hoanh Son range of mountains forms a natural barrier which once separated the Trinh and Nguyen lands in the 17th century and was the border of ancient Vietnam when Champa was at its peak.

Early morning fishing near Vinh.

Farmhouse near Can Loc

Above) Rice threshing between Ha Tinh and Cam Xuyen.

(*Above*) Road near Cam Xuyen.

(*Left*) Bicycles are used to transport virtually everything in Vietnam. These have no chains, and poles are attached to the handlebars for stability. Similar transport was used on the Ho Chi Minh trail.

People in Binh Tri Thien province believe that to die is to leave for another world. The relatives and people of the village want the dead to depart in contentment.

A traditional dance is performed by a local wise man to rid the household of evil spirits. The bearers, dressed in distinctive red uniforms, join in. The whole funeral ceremony is performed with great devotion and love, as the people prepare for the dead man's journey into another life. A beautiful funeral is important, since it means that the dead man's spirit will not return to bother the living.

(*Above*) The Betel ceremony still occurs in parts of rural Vietnam. There are three steps involved before permission is given for a wedding: a service is held, at which the boy's family ask the permission of the girl's family; the prospective husband carries betel nuts and sticky rice to the girl's house, followed by a long procession of village people; the gifts are offered to the family. If they accept, permission is given for the wedding. This ceremony is taking place in Truong Yen Village, Ha Nam Ninh province.

(*Opposite*) The band leads a funeral procession at Than Hoa.

(*Opposite*) Hien Luong – the 17th Parallel bridge.

(*Above*) Heavy rainfall sometimes causes extensive flooding in the Dong Hoi region.

(*Below*) Soil is loaded into boats for filling in bomb craters between Dong Hoi and the 17th Parallel bridge.

(*Below*) The reed jacket offers some protection from the rain.

The 17th Parallel Region

Binh Tri Thien province suffered greatly during the war, when massive amounts of bombs, napalm and defoliants destroyed the filao evergreen barriers which held back drifting sand from the rice fields. The area is subjected to massive flooding, which has hampered the filling-in of bomb craters and has allowed seawater to seep into good agricultural land, and there is still a problem from unexploded bombs; 900,000 have been unearthed since 1975-76 at a cost of over 100 casualties.

The Hien Luong bridge spanning the Ben Hai River on the 17th parallel once formed the dividing line between North and South Vietnam. From 1954 to 1975 it was completely closed—friends and families were isolated and not even mail passed between the North and South.

Several kilometres beyond the bridge is Con Tien, which in 1967 received indescribable pounding from warships and B52 bombers. The area almost ceased to exist, every thread of vegetation was charred. It was in this region that the McNamara defence line was to be built, stretching, two miles south of the demilitarized zone, right across to the Laotian border. Residents in the area still stockpile old Howitzer shells, which they sell for recycling.

Dong Ha, once an American air base, is where Highway No. 9 branches off in the A Luoi region. This valley part of the Truong Son range of mountains was devastated by bombs and defoliants. Now, after 18 years, the region is stunted. Once, over 150 animal species inhabited the area; most have completely disappeared. Highway No. 9, which transported the South Vietnamese during the invasion of Laos in March 1971, leads to the old American base at Khe Sanh. Still visible in the mountains surrounding the Bru Van Kieu hamlets are the branches of the Ho Chi Minh trail, 'Hanoi's road to victory', which carried military supplies from the north.

Beyond Dong Ha is Quang Tri, where a shell-damaged church pounded by the American Seventh Fleet reminds visitors of the devastation the area once experienced. Several old T54 Russian tanks are abandoned on the roadside.

A Bru Van Kieu minority village.

The Bru Van Kieu village in Huong Hoa (Khe Sanh) area is called 'Vil'. Each Vil comprises one or several Mu, each completely male dominated. They use 'Ray' or burnt-out jungle clearings to grow rice. These people helped during the war to maintain portions of the famous Ho Chi Minh trail, which passes through the western part of Binh Tri Thien, and fought fiercely against the Americans. Because of their great respect for Ho Chi Minh all Bru Van Kieus have adopted Ho as their first name.

Hue

Hue is the city where the Nguyen lords settled in the seventeenth century to make it the capital of Vietnam. Its enchanting location beside the Perfume River, where the songs of the boatwomen, 'Ho Mai Nhi' and 'Ho Mai Day', can be heard through the early morning mist, has always fascinated visitors. The river is still said to be scented by the Thach Xuong Bo shrub, which grows near its source. People come to see the antique charm of the Royal Tombs of the Nguyen Emperors Ming Mang, Khai Dinh, Tu Duc, Gia Long, Duc Duc, Dong Khanh and Ba Vanh. They come to see the grace of its beautiful girls, and to sample the mouth-watering cuisine. Many come to marvel at the splendour of the Imperial City and are outraged by the damage inflicted by warfare.

Hue was ruled in the 13th century by King Tran Anh Tong and for centuries it lay at the centre of the administrative unit known as Thuan Hoa. The capital was established at Phu Xuan village, where Nguyen Hue, the leader of the Tay Son rebellion, ascended the throne. It became the capital of the Nguyen Dynasty in 1802, when Nguyen Anh, later known as the Emperor Gia Long, became king.

It was during his reign that many parts of the Imperial City Dai Noi were built, including most of the Royal Citadel, Hoang Thanh, and the Forbidden Purple City, Tu Cam Thanh. The magnificent main gate, the Ngo Mon, appeared during the reign of Ming Manh, some years after the first Catholic riots had subsided in Hue.

The city was subjected to massive flooding for many years, the worst in 1844, when it was submerged under 10 m of water. 1866 was the year of the great rebellion, when thousands of soldiers and labourers building Tu Duc's tomb rebelled. The suburbs of the city were invaded by the French in 1833, when Tu Duc's funeral was in progress. In 1855, the year after Vietnam had become a French protectorate, the young Emperor, Ham Nghi, was forced to flee from the citadel on the approach of General Roussel's troops and the terrible slaughter that followed was accompanied by massive looting and burning.

There then followed a succession of Emperors, whose tombs are scattered throughout Hue district. Each was built during the king's lifetime and has three main features

representing the king's soul, a dedication to his memory and a list of his attributes. The last of these Nguyen kings, Bao Dai, abdicated in the Imperial City on 24 August 1945. The Japanese then took control and in 1954 it became part of South Vietnam.

A period of unrest followed sparked off by Buddhist demonstrations against the American occupation. Now visitors to the Thien Mu pagoda can see the car which transported Quang Duc to Saigon, where he burnt himself as a final protest against the Diem regime. Still standing in Hue are the Tu Dam and Dieude temples, where there were further monk suicides.

Hung introduces us to Hue, the old Imperial capital.

The Imperial City stands as a reminder of the excesses of the Vietnam War. During the four weeks of rebel occupation from the beginning of Tet 1968, US marines and Thieu's troops, helped by South Korean mercenaries, bombarded the Royal enclosures. The Seventh Fleet joined in the attack and even napalm and phosphorus bombs were hurled at the Forbidden City. The result was the removal of the yellow-starred flag and severe damage to countless historical structures. The area beyond the Thai Hoa Palace had been almost completely destroyed. To the Vietnamese this was a disaster akin to the razing of the Taj Mahal.

Sailing upstream on the Perfume River one comes across the Thien Mu pagoda, formerly called Linh Mu. This Buddhist seven-storey tower was built by Nguyen Hoang, the first governor of the southern court of Hue in 1601 using Cham bricks. Legend has it that an elderly goddess appeared there and recognized it as the foundation site for the capital city, hence its name, Elderly Goddess pagoda.

Beyond the tower is a huge bell cast in 1701. The entrance to the Buddhist sanctuary is guarded by six bizarre-looking genie and the inner enclosure contains a gilded statue of the Laughing Buddha enclosed in a glass case. Behind are three magnificent shining Buddhas, also surrounded by glass.

Inside the Buddhist sanctuary of the Thien Mu Pagoda.

The main entrance to the Imperial City – the Cua Ngo Mon (Noontime Gate). Built in 1834, during the reign of Ming Manh, it was repaired in the fifth year of Khai Dinh's reign in 1921. The Ngu Phung (Five Phoenix Building) stands on the top, overlooking the Great Rites Courtyard to the North, and the Ky Dai (King's Knight Tower) to the South. It is lit by the noonday sun.

The Imperial City

Visitors can look out from the Five Phoenix building on the top of the Noontime Gate, over the Thai Hoa Palace, and can imagine the splendour of the Royal ceremonies which took place in the Great Rites Courtyard. Two large griffins, their canopies slightly bullet-holed, stand watch. Frangipani blossoms to the sides of the Golden Water Bridge welcome the visitor with their fragrance.

This city, which was once one of Asia's greatest architectural treasures, is being restored with the help of UNESCO. The Purple Forbidden City, once off limits to aliens, is now largely non-existent; the two mandarin palaces have been restored, but the Dien Can Chanh, where the king would receive his mandarins, is just overgrown rubble. Beyond is the large expanse of waste ground which was once the site of the magnificent apartments of the queen.

Within the six-square-kilometre complex the Grandmother Palace still stands, its ornate roof now replaced by tin sheeting. Many of the original nine gates are in ruin, but the 'Female Gate', despite its blackened bullet-poxed walls, still has a certain appeal. The Hien Lam Cac temple gate and the magnificent dynastic urns are still an architectural wonder.

The golden throne of the Emperor
Gia Long stands on a dais in the
main hall of the Thai Hoa palace,
just inside the Imperial City.
Only the King and Princes were
allowed into this lavishly decorated
room.

(*Above*) The Thai Hoa palace.

(*Left*) One of the gryphons which stands to the left of the Great Rites Courtyard. Notice the bullet holes in the top of the canopy.

(*Below*) The Female Gate to the Imperial City – blackened and overgrown, but otherwise relatively unscathed by the war.

(*Above and Opposite*) The Dynastic Urns stand in front of the Temple Gate of Famous Souls (Hien Lam Cac). They were cast between 1835 and 1837, during the reign of the Emperor Ming Manh. These bronze masterpieces, engraved with scenes representing the Red, Perfume and Bach Dang Giang rivers, and the Hai Van Pass, weigh between 1,900 and 2,600 kilograms each. The central urn is the most ornate, and is dedicated to the Emperor Gia Long, the founder of the dynasty.

(*Above*) The tomb of Khai Dinh.

(*Opposite*) The Far Pavilion, at the site of the tomb of Ming Man

The Imperial Tombs can be reached by sailing up the Perfume River towards the rolling southern hills. These were built during the king's lifetime and each has three main features, representing the king's soul, a dedication to his memory and a list of his attributes. One of the most impressive is the tomb of Khai Dinh. Outside it is blackened by age, but inside there is an impressive arrangement of frescos inlaid with hundreds of thousands of colourful ceramic and glass fragments. There is a bronze statue of Khai Dinh, who ruled from 1916 until 1925, surrounded by sumptuous colourful ceramics.

The tomb of Ming Manh, 1820-40, is situated in Bang Viet village, Huong Tho district. It lies at the confluence of the Ta Trach and Huu Trach rivers, both tributaries of the Perfume River. Inside the mausoleum 40 small constructions are symmetrically set up with an imaginary west-east axis running from the front to the back end of the compound. One first comes across the Stele House—Bi Dinh—and can walk via a series of gates and temples to the catacomb itself.

Few visitors see all seven tombs, but the tomb of Tu Duc (1848-83), a very talented king, is worth a visit. He spent his leisure time in the complex which would become his mausoleum. There is an artificial lake, on the banks of which are two pavilions, Du Khiem and Xung Khiem. There are temples dedicated to the king, the king's mother, and even one dedicated to his concubines. The complex also contains the tomb of the queen Le Thien Anh, his official wife.

A duck herder on the road between Hue and Da Nang.

Oyster harvesting at the fishing village of Lang Co.

The Hai Van mountain range between Hue and Danang rises to around 6,000 feet in places and divides the Northern and Southern Trung Bo. This high mountain barrier must play an important role in shielding the southern area from the chilly north winds. From the Cul the lagoons of Cau Hai and Lang Co are just visible through the mist. Lang Co, at the northern foot of the pass, is a small fishing village where oysters are harvested. Delicious boiled oysters cooked over a mangrove charcoal fire are available from small stalls on the roadside.

(*Opposite*) A silk loom at Hoi An.

(*Below and Left*) Investigating fungal diseases of silkworms at SILKCO – the Union of Mulberry Silk Companies.

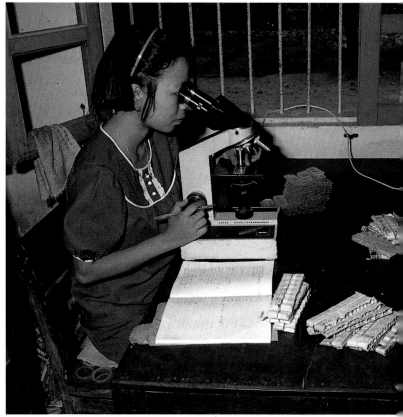

The textile industry in Danang has increased sixfold since 1975. This has been helped by the development of mechanical engineering shops, which build weaving looms and equipment for silk-worm breeding backed up with scientific research into the disease of silk worms. After the Vietnam War it had proved difficult to revive the weaving trade as most skilled weavers had left to seek a living elsewhere. Hoi An, 30 km from Danang, is famous as an old seaport, but also for its weaving trade. Walking through its narrow ancient streets the visitor can hear the clatter of weaving looms. Thanks to the return of skilled weavers there are now more than 600 looms in operation and Hoi An turns out over 4 million metres of cloth and silk fabrics every year.

Today Hoi An, probably one of the oldest towns in South-East Asia, has a population of around 55,000. Most are involved in the textile industry. Many Chinese have settled here. Because of its ideal geographical location it became an important marine trading centre in the fifteenth century. It is reported that the silk industry thrived in Hoi An when French merchants moved into the area when the north-south railway line reached Danang in 1930. The town became a scene of horror when the notorious South Korean Green Dragon brigade were moved there in 1965. All the local industries came to a standstill and have not recovered until recently. Life is now back to normal in Hoi An and visitors come to see the looms at work, the old Chinese architecture, the Japanese bridge and Fuc Kien pagoda. This was built by the Chinese and is dedicated to the Heavenly Lady, a Goddess who affords protection to mariners on their dangerous voyages.

The Heavenly Lady dominates the main altar in the Fuc Kien Pagoda at Hoi An.

(*Left, opposite*) The Huyen Khong cave

(*Right, opposite*) Inside the Tam Thai Temple

Dominating the landscape 8 km from the city of Danang is Ngu Hanh, the Marble Mountain, one of the five limestone peaks representing the five planets going around the sun.

The range contains mounts Moc (wood), Tho (earth), Kim (metal), Hoa (fire) and Thuy (water), representing the five basic components of the universe.

It was from these karst promontories that female guerilla fighters bombarded the American base at Nuoc Man and took potshots at enemy planes and helicopters.

Children at the base of the mountain will sell visitors joss sticks before they climb 156 stone steps to the Tam Thai temple. The Huyen Khong Cave beyond is an amazing Buddhist sanctuary with a huge stone Buddha and a large variety of Buddhist and Confucian figures. This once served as a base for the Hoa Vang and Phan Thanh Son female guerillas.

From the two observation points, Vong Hai and Vong Giang, at the summit, the city of Danang, and the countryside of Quang Nam, now a brilliant green, are again peaceful. During the war the filao forests had been flattened, allowing the encroaching sand to turn the province almost into a desert.

The swinging-basket method of irrigation, in use near Tam Ky.

Quang Nam Da Nang province experienced some of the heaviest bombardments during the Vietnam War. Now its capital Danang, once a small fishing village, has a new face. The massive American base is gone and barbed wire entanglements have been removed, but the old American Embassy still remains, a burnt-out reminder. Heading towards Highway No. 1 along Dien Bien Phu avenue, one cannot help thinking of the marines who landed in 1965 and frequented the bars now long gone but replaced with craft centres and weaving establishments.

In Duy Xuyen district there is a turn-off for the old Cham ruins of My Son and Tra Kieu along a route which suffered chemical defoliation. Few visitors get as far as Tra My district in the west, where minorities such as Kor, Mnong and Sedang still grow cinnamon. Near the border with Nghia Binh, the new filao pine plantations still fail to hold back the encroaching sand. The area is more fertile near Binh Son, where sugar cane plantations flourish. To the west is Tra Bong, famous for its huge forests of podocarpus and bamboo, which once hid guerilla fighters from the French and American troops. The people of Binh Son remember well the Ba Gia victory they had against the puppet army and US forces, and the fight of the Van Tuong people and liberation army against a massive US marine attack.

The people in this area have never had an easy life. The annual drought between March and July means that water must be shifted from one level to another using primitive swinging baskets or large norias (irrigation wheels). No remnants of the American base at Quang Nhai remain, now the only sound comes from the large presses at the sugar cane factory.

Around Mo Duc tobacco plantations flourish, and further south, lush rice paddies line the roadside. Bamboo hedges shield the villages and the newly grown coconut palms whistle in the wind. Despite the devastation from warfare and typhoons, gardens are loaded with guava, jackfruits, avocado pears and coconuts. Coconut palms, some grossly wounded, provide good protection from the sweltering heat of the midday sun. Children with smiling faces, who do not remember the 30 years of war against France and the USA, wave to strangers as they pass by.

The salt marshes surrounding the port of Sa Huynh are back in full swing, producing 60,000 tons of salt a year. Small stalls selling brushes and ropes made from coconut bristles line the roadway to the small hamlet of Tam Quan. The coconut plantations near Phu Cat, once a military base, provide valuable copra oil. Cat Hanh village, where 80 per cent of the houses had been destroyed by American and Korean troups, has been completely rebuilt, but the land remains infertile still unrecovered from toxic chemicals. The Thi Nai lagoon near Quy Nhon is producing massive numbers of shrimps, and carambola trees are now dotted over the landscape. Hardy peasants with black enamelled teeth cultivate the rice fields. Old Cham towers are seen on the horizon, reminders of a bygone era. Quy Nhon is now a sleepy port, a far cry from the days when military vehicles rumbled through its streets.

Sugar cane being sold near Quang Ngai.

A rice field in Nghia Binh province. Note the Cham tower in the background.

It is common practice among the peasants of Nghia Binh province to enamel their teeth.

A peasant rebellion in the 18th century started by Nguyen Huu Cau brought fear into the hearts of the aristocracy; although imprisoned in 1751 his words had spread far and wide. A great movement rose up, that of the Tay Son in Binh Dinh province (central Vietnam) in 1771. This was led by the genius strategist Nguyen Hue, who rallied the people from as far away as An Khe district, Kontum province.

Together with his brothers Nguyen Lu and Nguyen Nhac, he was determined to stop the cruel exploitation of the peasants by the Trinh and Nguyen lords. They adopted a policy of 'Take from the rich and give to the poor', which considerably popularized their cause, resulting in the founding of a huge peasant army. It was not long before they had overthrown the Trinh lords in the north and the Nguyen lords in the south.

Nguyen Anh had obtained reinforcements from Siam led by Generals Chieu Tang and Chieu Suong. This 20,000-strong army was supported by 30 war junks. The Tay Son fleet lured them into a trap near present-day My Tho and gained one of the most brilliant victories in Vietnamese history. The battle became known as Rach Gam-Xoai (20 January 1785). A resounding victory against the Le kings and their 200,000 strong Manchu army reinforcements on the site of present-day Hanoi followed (January 1789).

Nguyen Hue became a national hero and decrees were issued to lighten tax burdens and improve the life of the peasants. To celebrate the Tay Son era, on the fifth day of the first lunar month a festival is held at Nguyen Hue museum, where the hero's statue looks out over mountains named after him and his two brothers.

The Quang Trung-Nguyen Hue museum.

Tay Son martial arts spring from the same national source which includes whole sets of exercises such as Ngoc Tran, Lao Mai, Than Dong, perfected since the 18th century. A demonstration of Tay Son Vo Si occurs on special occasions at the Quang Trung-Nguyen Hue museum. The students receive lessons from a master, who teaches them each stroke. Some strokes are kept secret and taught only to the patriotic-minded students who, in the opinion of the master, are entirely devoted to their fellow Vietnamese. In Binh Dinh area a famous Wushu instructor has taught students for over half a century. The people of Binh Dinh are well known for their love of martial arts. Nguyen Lu, Nguyen Hue's younger brother, devised the 'cockfight' method, noting that in a fight the larger cock can be beaten by a smaller one. He developed a method which allowed men of small stature to defeat larger adversaries. Tay Son martial arts has had a good effect on the physical and moral culture of the young in the same way as it helped Nguyen Hue's troops to become a redoubtable force.

Preparing for the performance.

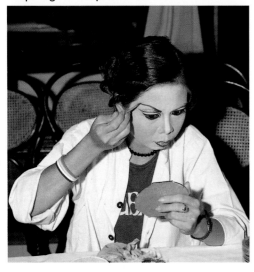

Vo Si Thua is the Director of the Dao Tan theatre. He is one of the men who has contributed most to the Tuong opera, and is a foremost exponent of the art.

The Nghia Binh Classical Opera Theatre was named after renowned playwright Dao Tan. He was born in the Quy Nhon area and was an outstanding poet as well as a classical opera artist. Even during the war of resistance to the French and the Vietnam War, classical opera stars still performed and improved their art. The actor Vo Si Thua is one of the men who has contributed most to the development of the Tuong. Near Phuoc Van travellers venture to Vinh Thanh, a small village where Dao Tan was born, to see the Tuong performed. Tuong made its appearance on the stage as far back as the first independent royal dynasties (end of the 10th and early 11th centuries). It was not until the Tran dynasty that the Tuong was firmly established. It reached its peak during the reign of Tran D[...] Tong (1341-69). A Tuong script is an adaptation of an ol[...] story or book, taken from Chinese history. Tuong art is sai[...] by the Vietnamese to be that of Ta Than (portrayal of th[...] human soul). The colour of the skin of the performers i[...] significant. Red is for honest people, blue for mountaineer[...] orange for fishermen, white with black for traitors. [...] dragon's beard indicates a king or nobleman. Eye sockets o[...] different shapes indicate different characters. Vo Si Thua, th[...] director of the opera theatre, says 'that the strength of Tuon[...] in Vietnam can be compared to mercury, once it falls on th[...] ground it can penetrate everywhere'.

The Cham people built up the ancient state of Champa, which arose in the late 2nd century AD. At this time it had four main centres. In the middle provinces of Vietnam there was 'Amaravati', extending from Binh Tri Thien right through Quang Nam Da Nang, and 'Vijaya' in Nghia Binh province. In the southern provinces other centres included 'Kauthara' in Phu Khanh, and 'Panduranga' in Thuan Hai province.

Very few Cham people now live in the middle provinces apart from scattered settlements in Nghia Binh. Most are confined to the old southern centres, but some have radiated into An Giang province in the Mekong Delta.

The Kingdom of Champa reigned until the 18th century, when the last king, Po Klong Khuan, died. Many Cham people then left Vietnam and settled in Kampuchea.

Vestiges of Cham culture in the form of ancient towers are found all over the central and some of the southern provinces. Their towers, which were built of cubes all made of red brick, had a central square section and a pointed roof rather like a stupa. Many decorative motifs, often of lotus flowers, men fighting or wild beasts and monsters, are stuck or engraved on their sides. Even now, we don't know what type of glue was used by these people to give such invisible solid linkages between the bricks.

In all, 128 important vestiges of ancient Cham culture have been discovered in Vietnam. Some of the most important archeologically are the Myson ruins 28 km west of Tra Kieu in Quang Nam Da Nang province. Myson was built during the reign of King Bhadravarman and called Srisanabhadresvara. The whole complex was heavily bombed by the US air force. The Tra Kieu remains south of Danang were the site of the capital of the Kingdom of Champa from the 7th to the 10th centuries. All that is left is a series of old trenches beside the Thu Bon River. Famous in this area is Dong Duong, built during the reign of King Indravarman II, where there are still remains of old shrines and monasteries. There are also the remains of other Amaravati structures, the best known in this province being the Khuong My towers, Chien Dan and Bang An.

During the 11th century the distinct style of Cham art was known as Chanh Lo, and some examples have been discovered in the Quang Ngai area.

The Yang Mun style found in Gia Lai, Kontum province, was formed during the decline in Cham art at the beginning of the 15th century.

When the Kingdom of Champa was situated in Nghia Binh province, the Thap Mam style, which was influenced by Dai Viet and Khmer art, originated. The best examples of this style are seen at Binh Dinh district, just outside Quy Nhon, where the three majestic towers date from the 11th to the 14th century.

The museum of Cham culture built in 1915 was started under the patronage of the Ecole Française D'Extreme Orient, Hanoi, in Danang city, and has exhibits of Cham figures dating from the 4th to the 14th century.

Cham statues from Thap Mam, Nghia Binh province, in the Cham Museum at Da Nang. On the left is the goddess Than Siva; on the right, Ho Phap Dvarapala.

ham towers in Binh Dinh district.

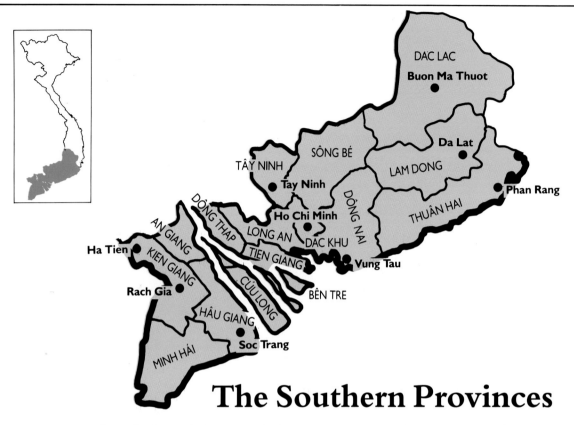

The Southern Provinces

At the time when the French first invaded Vietnam in 1858, the gateway to the southern provinces at the Cu Mong Pass lay in Cochinchina. It was through this gateway in the 17th century that the mighty Tay Son peasant armies of Nguyen Hue marched to a confrontation with Nguyen Anh.

Throughout history the southern provinces have never been a peaceful place. In 1833, when Ho Chi Minh, the capital, was called Gia Dinh, the citadel was attacked by Le Van Khoi and later razed to the ground by Ming Manh's troops in a tremendous battle which raged in 1835.

The revolutionary writer Nguyen Dinh Chieu, born in Saigon, and Ton Duc Thang, from Long Xuyen, did everything in their power to resist when French rule came to the South in 1859. By 1910 the city had become a trading port and large ships from Europe and Far Eastern countries sailed up the deep, wide estuary. Other southern areas had been linked by roads and a railway extending from Saigon to Nha Trang had been built.

Opposition to French rule heightened in the 1930-45 period, culminating in the Nam Ky insurrection in November 1940. For the next five years the South was under the double yoke of the French and Japanese. Although independence came in September 1945, the French, together with the British, occupied Saigon in 1947. Trouble brewed during President Diem's term of office, first from the Hoa Hao armies in 1955, and then from Buddhist uprisings against his regime in the 1960s. Even his generals turned against him in 1963, and during the coup d'état organized by 'Big Minh' (Duong Van Minh) he and his brother were assassinated. During Thieu's reign the southern provinces became a battlefield, and the countryside emptied as peasants fled from the American bombs. The land had never witnessed such devastation and after the NLF tanks rumbled into Saigon in 1975, a million women were left without husbands.

Now it is difficult to imagine such atrocities in provinces blessed with such natural beauty and friendly, smiling people. The American warships which once occupied the magnificent bays of Cam Ranh, Hon Khoi and Dai Lanh have long gone. Peace has returned to the cool mountain air of Dalat and Buon Ma Thuot. The mountain tribes, the Mnong, continue to hunt elephants, and the Ede, Kodang, Bahnar, Giarai, Ma and K'hor continue to grow coffee, tea, pepper, rice and bamboo in the rich red basaltic soils. No longer are there any Australian soldiers in Vung Tau, their place having been taken by Russian oil experts. Nha Trang is once again a holiday resort, where people come to worship Ponagar in the old Kauthara Cham towers overlooking the Cai River. The raffia and rubber plantations of Dong Nai thrive and the Cham people continue to cultivate rice alongside the old Thap Mam towers at Phan Rang. Peace and solitude have returned to the Mekong Delta despite a Pol Pot invasion in An Giang and other border provinces with Kampuchea during 1977-78.

Dai Lanh fishing village near the start of the Deo Ca Pass, about 80 kilometres north of Nha Trang.

Quy Nhon

Further south from Quy Nhon the road passes through the Cu Mong pass. Built mainly from granite it stretches through shrubby savannah terrain. At Song Cau, after the plains of Binh Dinh and Phu Yen, it skirts the blue-green sea. Towards the plain of Tuyan there are many sugar cane plantations, and tobacco flourishes in the area in heavy compacted soil which favours the dark, rich, high-nicotine stock. In the Tuy Hoa area north of Deo Ca are well-cultivated rice fields. In the region a one-kilometre bridge, one of the longest in Vietnam, crosses the Da River. As early as the 1930s a massive irrigation system and the Dong Cam dam had been built in the area. The land has now recovered from its considerable bombardment during the war. Many coconut groves had been destroyed because they were safe guerilla bases, acted as efficient watch towers and were often used for machine-gun installations. The green fortresses have largely been replaced through extensive replanting programmes instigated after 1975. Further south the road winds towards Nha Trang via Ninh An and Ninh Tho through the Deo Ca pass.

The fishermen of Nghia Binh province say that the fishing stock floats. They know full well that the currents of Nghia Binh flow from the north during the southern monsoon and take the reverse course during the winter. The fish then 'float' southwards. The chief species caught are types of horse mackerel, sprats, sperlings and flying fish. The coastline of Nghia Binh was very well policed during the Vietnam War because of supplies being sent south to the Viet Cong to supplement those arriving along the Ho Chi Minh trail.

Mending the fishing nets at the village of Cua Be, near Nha Trang.

Buon Ma Thuot is reached via a pitted, tortuous road branching off from Highway No. 1 leading to Nha Trang. The road in this part of Dac Lac province passes the thatched long houses of the Ede minority. Buon Ma Thuot, capital of the province, has an interesting market, ethnic minority museum and a most amazing war monument in the town centre. There are lots of beer parlours and small cafés where the visitor can drink coffee grown locally in Doan Ket co-operative. Very few tourists have visited the area and those that have are mainly Russian delegations researching coffee cultivation techniques. This town received the full onslaught of three North Vietnamese divisions during the Vietnam War, the artillery attack flattening most of the coffee plantations surrounding the town. Thanks to the hard work of the locals and the rich red basalt soil in the area they have been replanted together with other crops such as rubber, tea and pepper. Water is abundant in the area from a large network of rivers which empty into the Mekong via the Serepok and Eakrong.

(*Above*) The first Russian-made tank to enter Buon Ma Thuot: March, 1975.

(*Right*) I wonder if he wears it every day?

(*Opposite*) The statue commemorates those who died during the War in Ea Nop district, Dac Lac province.

Don Village

Don Village is situated in Ea Sup district, Dac Lac province, 45 km from Buon Ma Thuot. The minority here, predominantly Mnong, are elephant hunters. The area has been known for its wild elephants ever since the Dong Dau period, 3,000 years ago. The villagers use their 56 tame elephants in the round-up. Recently, together with hunters from Krong Ana village, they have trapped a white elephant. This is the third to be caught in this district; the second was confiscated by President Ngo Dinh Diem and sent to the United States in the 1960s. Some of the elephants caught by the Mnong have ended up in western zoos and they often have a price tag of over one million dong. The village often provides elephants for important ceremonies such as the elephant parade in Buon Ma Thuot to mark the tenth anniversary of its liberation (March 1985). The parade involved 33 large elephants carrying highly ornamental howdahs marching 11 abreast in rows of three, with three young elephant following their mothers. Many are still taken to the Tay Son festival in Quy Nhon.

(*Top, opposite*) An example of a long house, built by the Mnong people in Don village.

(*Bottom, opposite*) Mnong children. The 'gun' made from a reed.

(*Left*) A Mnong elephant hunter in Don village.

The Mnong long house is often 40 metres long and is supported by stilts. Several families live in one house and share its contents. Huge ropes used in the elephant hunts dangle from the roof, dried frog and snake meat adorns the walls. These are remedies often used against dyspepsia and rheumatics. The human placenta is dried and powdered and become part of the ingredients of Ha Sa Dai Tao, used to treat broncho-pulmonary and rheumatic disorders.

A Western visitor to a Mnong settlement is given Ruou Can, fermented rice wine, which he drinks through long bamboo straws from a Che container at the same time as the Chief and elders. To add to the atmosphere the visitors will be entertained by a variety of Cong percussion instruments, Khah, Hlue Khok, Hlue Lhiang, Mdu Khok, to the accompaniment of a Ngor drum.

The village has extensive grasslands and sugar cane plantations for feeding the animals. Other minorities in the area, Ede, Gia Rai, Lao, Khmer and Thai, help the Mnong to farm the red basaltic soil of the highlands. This fertile land provides cotton, coffee, tea, rice, sesame, beans and ground nuts, which are sold in the market in Buon Ma Thuot. The forests are exploited for their timber: Trac, Lim, Tau, Gu Cam and Mun. The mountain tribes are excellent hunters and often supplement their diets with flying squirrel, peacocks and pheasants. They know their forests well and some are experts on phytotherapy (herb medicine). They gather the green leaves of Mo Qua, which are used to heal wounds. Cinnamon is collected and used as a circulatory and respiratory stimulant. An interesting concoction is Xong, which is prepared from lemon and grapefruit leaves, bamboo, artemisia, ocimum, perilla and elsholtzis, and is brewed back at the long house by boiling all the ingredients in water. The smoke is inhaled and is a treatment used for influenza.

Many minority people inhabit the province of Dac Lac, including Ede, Mnong, Gia Rai, Xodang, Bih, Ma, Bu Tonly, Khmer, Bahnar, Cham, Churu, Raglai, Bulay, Van Kieu, Muong, Hoa, Tay, Thai, Nung and Dao. Tua village of the Ede minority has long houses arranged in adminstrative units called 'Buon'. The ladders at the entry to the houses are sometimes elaborately carved with symbols of the moon, elephant tusks, and breasts. Each long house of Sang Dok is often 50–60 metres long and accommodates five families. They survive by growing sweet potatoes, manioc and maize. They keep livestock and weave cloth. They even have their own school.

A view of Nha Trang over the Cai River. In the distance can be seen the White Buddha – Thich Ca of the Long Son Pagoda.

(*Left*) The statue of Ponagar in the Cham Temple at Nha Trang.

(*Right, opposite*) Cham ruins at Phan Ran

(*Left, opposite*) Cham people planting rice make
splendid contrast in their colourful headscarves t
the almost fluorescent green of the young ric
fields. This is the Bac Binh district, in the province o
Thuan Ha

Nha Trang is known not only for its splendid sandy beaches but also for its Cham towers and Giant white Buddha. This stands at Longson pagoda, built in 1963 to commemorate the successful struggle against the Diem regime. From the Xom Bong bridge in Nha Trang the famous Cham towers containing a statue of Ponagar can be seen. She is sometimes called Mother Earth and also Uma and has been represented as a woman with breasts bursting with milk and a generous belly. To the Cham people she is a heavenly lady who taught them agricultural techniques, fishing and medicine. Pilgrims flock to visit the temple on the 1st and 15th of each lunar month. The main Merian festival is held there on the 20th of the third lunar month.

The Cham people who live in Phu Khanh and Thuan Hai province belong to the clan known as the Cau (Areca). The Kingdom of Champa, which came into being in the late 2nd Century AD, consists of two important centres seen in this area — The Kauthara in Phu Khanh and the Panduranga in Thuan Hai. One can often see Cham people walking down the road, especially from the Cam Ranh area (once a military base) along the road to Phan Rang. Two Cham towers stand at Phan Rang on the side of Highway No. 1.

The Cham people are good fishermen and experts at building dams and reservoirs, irrigation channels and turning arid land into lush fields. On the plain of Phan Rang the remains of Cham hydraulic works such as Maren and the Chakling dam are seen. Cham villages are noted for their

neatly arranged rows of houses, which lie well hidden. The Cham in Thuan Hai have adopted the old Islamic doctrine and are called Ba Ni. The traditional Kate festival is held in the last months of each year. The Cham men then dress in white garments. They visit ancestors' graves and pay tribute to the spirits of their ancestors and the God Kut. They perform folk songs and dances — Ca Mang, Pa Choa and Pideu. Westerners are excluded from their festivities.

Dong Nai province (Deer Land) is formed from the merger of three former provinces, Ba Ria, Ben Hoa and Long Khanh. It is well known for its 40,000 hectares of rubber plantations. As the road winds south towards Vung Tau massive plantations can be seen in the Long Thanh area. The very dry climate is exceptional for the growth of hevea rubber, which is highly disease-resistant. The plantations were created by the French over 50 years ago on Terres Rouges soil. Some plantations are backward due to the harmful effects of the war. The first latex is collected when the trees are five or six years old by topping in the early morning and collecting in cups in the evening. The latex is coagulated with acetic acid in the factory and then passed through rolling mills to produce sheets of prime rubber.

(*Right*) A rubber plantation.

(*Opposite*) Raffia drying in Dong Hai province.

Vung Tau is a popular holiday resort 125 km from Ho Chi Minh. It was a small fishing village in the early 20th century. When the French arrived they built a beach resort and called it Cap St Jacques. The 100,000 or so population live on fishing and handicraft manufacture. The fishing fleet arrives at about 6 o'clock in the morning and unloads mountains of fish of all sizes and baskets full of shrimps; the fisheries in the area are tremendously productive. A new breeding centre for grey shrimps has been set up (June 1987) at Con Dao with a very efficient water circulation and feed processing system which after only one month's operation produced over 1 million fry. Ben Da fishing village a few kilometres from the front beach is the place to go to observe fish of all descriptions being dried, skinned, sectioned, and salted. The locals are charming and extremely healthy looking, and children every-where will cry 'Lien Xo, Lien Xo' (Russian! Russian!). They naturally think every white-faced individual is Russian, probably because of the massive oil installations off the coast in this region which are run by the USSR. Just off shore in the Bai Dau area leg-rowing fishermen pull in their nets. Close to this area is Bach Dinh, or Villa Blanche, a former summer residence of Bao Dai—the last emperor of Vietnam's Nguyen Dynasty. Built in the early 20th century it became the summer house of Nguyen Van Thieu, former president of South Vietnam. From the grounds the visitor can have a marvellous panoramic view of Vung Tau. Just around the corner where the fishing fleet dock is the reclining Buddha Temple or 'Nirvana Meditation Street Temple'— Niet Ban Tinh Xa. This was built in 1969 and is one of the most beautiful temples in the area. The main beach area in Vung Tau is worth a visit. This is where Australian servicemen used to relax on leave during the war. Photographers sporting Russian cameras are eager to picture tourists sitting under colourful umbrellas eating sugar cane and pineapples sold by vendors with conical hats.

(*Opposite*) The Reclining Buddha.

(*Below*) Waiting for the fishing fleet.

Lam Dong province is important for growing maize. The road is littered with peasants threshing rice. Large lorries laden with wood barge their way down from the forests in Da Huoai district. Towards Bao Loc area it is invariably raining. The rainy season in this area lasts six months, from May to October. The climate is particularly favourable for growing tea. The April tea farm named after the 30 April 1975 Liberation of Saigon is one of the largest. Rice grows prolifically towards Dalat.

(*Left*) Hoeing the weeds in the maize field.

(*Opposite*) Rice planters

(*Above*) A hamlet near Bao Loc.

(*Left*) Picking tea at the April Tea Far

The Ma minority are found in Lam Dong province. The majority live in the Bao Loc area and in Di Linh district. They have a population of about 30,000. Ma people speak Vietnamese although they have their own language.

The Ma tribe consists of many subdivisions, Maxop, Ma To, Ma Hoang, Ma Krung, Ma Ngan. They live on agriculture, growing rice, corn, pumpkins, squash, tobacco and cotton. They harvest two rice crops a year, in late July and late October. Many now work in the tea and coffee plantations, but they still hunt and fish. They live in a small village called a Bon and the women are married at the early age of 15 or 16. They believe that everything is controlled by a supernatural force called Yang. They worship Yang Hin—God of the House—Yang Koi—God of Rice—and Yang Bri—God of the Forest.

Weddings are normally held in Vietnam in autumn and winter, especially on the approach of Tet. On the day a delegation arrives to fetch the bride. It is headed by a Chu Hon (Master of Ceremonies). On arrival at the gate of the reception area firecrackers are let off, and during the reception a representative of the bridegroom's family rises and makes a little speech, the gist of which is to 'ask for the bride'. The bridegroom, accompanied by his groomsmen, goes into the bride's chamber. He presents her with a bouquet, and both go out into the reception room to be presented to the participants to the ceremony: relatives, friends, neighbours. The Master of Ceremonies formally announces their union. It is not uncommon for the bride to change into another dress in her formal changing room which is just off the reception area.

Certain rituals are observed in a country wedding in Vietnam. The preliminary contact is designated by various names: Cham Ngo (contact with the house), Dam Mat (getting to know the features) or Van Danh (asking the name). The horoscopes of both parties are often compared. A Betrothal Ceremony often follows, when the young man's family would bring areca nuts, betel leaves, tea and maybe wine and cakes. Some of these gifts are traditionally returned to the sender — a gesture called Lai Qua; the implication is that formal ties have been established.

The K'hor minority live mainly on the plateau in Lam Dong province. The group has many subdivisions, including Co Don, Ta Ngau, Chil, Lat, Mang To, To La, Nop and Sre. Their houses are built on stilts with floors of the crushed stems of Buong or Mai woven into a sturdy base. They grow rice, beans, calabashes, pumpkins and tobacco, which they sell in Dalat market.

Some K'hor still follow the ancient custom of using hollowed-out tree trunks for coffins. Their God is Ndu, the creator; some are ancestor worshippers, and a few even became Catholics during French colonial times. They are very fond of musical instruments, brass gongs, bamboo flutes, horns and lutes. Today they have formed large co-operatives, many have gone to University in Ho Chi Minh and among their ranks there are members of the National Assembly.

The faces of Da Lat — Viet, Ma and K'hor.

Although visitors are taken to Cu Chi as a deliberate reminder of the war, all that remains above ground is a rusting American M41 tank. Below ground the whole countryside is riddled with over 300 km of tunnels which were once strongholds for the Viet Cong. Combined American and Australian war effort failed, in operations such as Crimp (January 1966) and Cedar Falls (January 1967), to make much impression on the area. The tunnels were used for concealing troops, arms and food supplies and for planning major offensives. There were even hospitals and training areas underground.

Ho Chi Minh City

Most tourists fly into Ho Chi Minh City in the sleek-bodied jets of Air France. Approaching Tan Son Nhut airport, piles of old Huey helicopters, anti-blast walls and rusting B52 bombers come into view. After the disorganized form-filling, Japanese microbuses carry visitors into the city. Those looking for reminders of the war will be hard pressed, but the very observant may notice the sign MACV–'Military Assistance Command Vietnam' on one of the underpasses. Tourists are surprised at the large number of small motorcycles in the city centre. A few may be astonished by the teeming hordes of bicycles and pedicabs which swarm down the tree-lined boulevards.

These days Ho Chi Minh, although having an air of neglect, has a slightly Western feel to it. Many bars are re-opening and at night there is the faint sound of dance music. Compared to Bangkok it has a village-type atmosphere, the bars are well hidden and the discos play music from the sixties.

After the decadence of the West, it is in some ways like stepping into a time machine and finding oneself in another era. One wonders what it might have been like if one could exaggerate the time warp and travel back to the days when it was a trade centre called Dong Na in lower Cochinchina. According to old manuscripts, the Saigon River was swarming with crocodiles which made noises like buffaloes, which was the reason why it later became known as Ben Thanh (the landing stage of buffaloes). Now Ben Thanh is a name given to a market selling virtually any luxury item, including transistor radios, refrigerators, cameras, calculators and other items from many Western countries.

The old name Saigon was first used by Le Quy Don in the 1728-85 period and many who live there now still call it by this name. From the top of the Doc Lap, formerly the Caravelle Hotel, used extensively by journalists during the war, there is a magnificent panoramic view of the city. The street running towards the Catholic basilica was a fashionable shopping area in the 1950s and was crammed with sleazy night spots during the American occupation. Today Dong Khoi, formerly known as Rue Catinat and To Do, is dotted with tourist handicraft shops selling lacquerware, pottery, bamboo, rattan and rush articles.

The word Rex can still be seen on the Ben Thanh Hotel, where delectable hostesses entertain foreigners in a nightclub with definitely no hanky panky to follow. Beyond the Cathedral is the Reunification Hall where, on 30 April 1975, the last Saigon President, General Duong Van Minh, and his cabinet surrendered to the Vietnamese liberation forces. From its third floor visitors can look out on to Le Duan Boulevard, which, on liberation day, was festooned with NLF tanks before they smashed through the main gates of the Presidential Palace.

There are many signs of industrial improvement in the city. Thousands of new jobs have been created in textiles, crafts, food processing, bicycle production, chemical, electrical and ship-building. The number of skilled workers is increasing, but there is still a drastic shortage of raw materials. To cope with the large population expansion there has been a rapid growth in health care; there are now 35 hospitals, 80 health stations, hundreds of maternity care centres, and six orphanages.

A typical tourist circuit of the city may visit the old American Embassy, now an oil office, the war crimes museum, which reminds visitors of the horrors of Vietnam's various wars, the new youth school and a detoxification centre for drug addicts. Tourists are often taken to China town, Cholon. The Hoa, Chinese traders, were allowed to settle in the south in the 17th century by the Nguyen princes and gradually integrated into the Vietnamese community, but set up their own colony Cholon (big market). The huge market, Binh Tay, in the heart of China town is a good place for visitors to buy knick-knacks. Culinary tastes are well catered for by the Lam Son, Vinh Loi and Arc En-Ciel restaurants, which serve delicious eels, frogs and wild game followed by seven-course beef.

When Saigon was opened as a port in 1860, one year after it was seized by the French, the Chinese community of Cholon had expanded considerably. The French had exploited the southern peasantry with the help of the Hoa, and laid the foundations for trade routes leading to Saigon. Saigon became the pearl of the Orient and Cholon the centre of trade for the delta.

(*Top*) Bicycle spares are plentiful enough — if you can afford them . . .

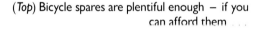

. . . and there is no shortage of bicycle repair shops (*right*).

The Ram Thang Gien Buddhist Festival at the Chinese Temple in Cholon (Ho Chi Minh's Chinese Quarter).

(*Right*) One of the main altars of the temple in Nguyen Trai Street, built in the 1830s by the Cantonese community. It is dedicated to the Heavenly Lady Thien Hau, who is the protector of the Chinese people, particularly when they are travelling on water. On the roof of the temple are rows of sculptured figurines depicting ancient Chinese folk tales.

(*Opposite Page*) Notre Dame – the Catholic cathedral in Ho Chi Minh's Cathedral Square. Approximately 100,000 Catholics were brutally murdered in the 19th century, but the religion has been increasing in popularity for many years.

(*Below*) Funeral musicians in Cholon.

The Drum dance – one of the traditional folk dances that are very popular with tourists at the Rex Hotel.

(*Right*) The Dong Nai ceramics factory produces 200,000 pieces a year, many of which are exported.

(*Below Right*) The reed mats are being made at Orphanage Number One, Ho Chi Minh City. In addition to their academic studies, the children spend two or three hours a day learning a variety of skills. There are six orphanages in the City, selling many of the handicraft goods they produce through the local markets.

(*Below Left*) An artist at the Son Mai Lam Son Lacquerware factory. The lacquer is a sap, obtained from the lacquer trees in the Vinh Phu district. Thirteen or fourteen coats are applied to a plywood base, which is then either painted or inlaid with eggshell or mother-of-pearl. The surface is then finished by rubbing it with a cuttle bone on a special type of charcoal.

Market stalls in the Cholon quarter. There are thirty-two large markets in Ho Chi Minh City, at which you can buy a wide range of goods, including many imported luxury items. State trade shops have been opened in an attempt to reduce the thriving black market.

The Cathedral at Tay Ninh

The Cathedral at Tay Ninh is the headquarters of the Cao Dai religion. Cao Daism was founded by Ngo Van Chieu in 1925.

During a seance held in 1919 he made contact with a spirit that identified itself as Cao Dai, or 'The Supreme Being'. Later, in another seance in Saigon, he was told to symbolize the 'Supreme Being' with a large eye emitting bright rays of light. Le Van Trung, who joined the sect, replaced Ngo Van Chieu as its leader in 1926. On 7 October 1926 it became a formal religion, with the primary aim of uniting other great religions such as Confucianism, Christianity, Toaism, Spirit Worship and Buddhism. Much of its doctrine stems from Mahayana Buddhism. In hierarchical order, the head of the religion is Cao Dai, as symbolized by the eye emitting radiant light, seen on the front of the Cathedral and on all Cao Dai temples.

Below the Supreme Being are the three great saints—Confucius, Buddha and Laotse. The high category of saints include Quan Am—the Buddhist goddess of mercy—the Chinese warrior—Quan Cong, and Moses. Other saints include Sun Yat Sen, Jeanne d'Arc, Victor Hugo and the French admiral Duclos.

By the 1930s, the Tam-Ky-Pho-Do sect, another name for Cao Daism, had developed a definite hierarchical structure. Its head was Pope Le Van Trung and below him were cardinals, archbishops and priests. Women were welcomed into the sect. During this period in Tay Ninh a colourful and architecturally bizarre cathedral was constructed. A Cao Dai army was organized with the assistance of French military advisers.

The main sect divided into many others which spread over the southern part of Vietnam. Soon, there were different sects in Ben Tre, Rach Gia, Bac Lieu, Tan An and Can Tho. Many were mistrusted by the French administration and during the Indo-China War some Cao Dai cathedrals were destroyed.

After the war many more sprung up and Cao Daists had more freedom. Meanwhile His Holiness Le Van Trung, who had taken the name of Thuong Trung Nhuri, had died and been replaced by a new Pope—Pham Cong Tac. Cao Daism developed over a million adherents and the headquarters of 'The Holy See' became the cathedral at Tay Ninh, about 50 miles north-west of Saigon.

Inside the cathedral a notice in several languages asks visitors to remove their shoes. A large painting of Cao Dai saints greets visitors to the vestibule. One is Ton Trung Sen—the creator of the Chinese Republic—i.e. Sun Yat Sen. Another is Nguyen Binh Khiem, a Vietnamese nobleman, and the other is Nguyet Tan Chon Nhon—who proved to be Victor Hugo.

Inside, the dozen pillars on each side are encircled by brightly painted dragons and the floor is arranged on nine levels, each one slightly above the other. Members of the faith are vegetarians and they refrain from chewing betel or observing other wordly practices.

The ceremony inside the cathedral can be watched from the balcony. Two lines of figures file into the temple accompanied by a band comprising one-stringed fiddles and cymbals and a small choir. The figures are dressed in different colours, which are determined by the branch of the faith concerned. The Confucianist branch concerned with the rites wear purple robes—the symbol of authority.

The Taoists wear azure gowns—the symbol of tolerance. The Buddhists wear yellow robes—Saffron yellow being the symbol of virtue. The elders are in white.

Periodically a bell sounds, and the congregation bows low towards the ever-seeing eye of the main altar. To a Westerner's eye the ceremony seems to be very bizarre, but no one could doubt the sincerity of its advocates.

The interior of the Tay Ninh cathedral.

The Mekong Delta

To the south of Ho Chi Minh City are nine provinces criss-crossed with thousands of kilometres of waterways. The mighty Mekong River, whose arteries and capillaries reticulate through 4 million hectares, brings in 500 billion cubic metres of water annually. During the 16th century people began to colonize the Giong silted areas. They built fishing villages and gradually tamed the waters using dykes and irrigation channels. They drained the marshy land and constructed transportation canals. The biggest were Thoai Ha and Vinh Te, linking An Giang and Kien Giang provinces.

New roads were constructed by the French helped by finance from Hoa traders and later improved during the American occupation. The result is that Ho Chi Minh City is now linked via Highway No. 4 with the western part of Dong Thap, An Giang and even the eastern part of Minh Hai. The produce of the Mekong granaries eventually ends up in the markets of Ho Chi Minh via the ferry crossings at Ben Tre to My Tho, Dong Thap to My Thuan, Cuu Long to My Thuan and Hau Giang to Cuu Long.

Rice is the main crop of the Delta—Lua Thuat, sticky rice, and Lua Canh, non-sticky rice. Monoculture is a thing of the past and even the previously badly flooded areas of An Giang now yield two crops per year. The Botany Department of Can Tho University has researched better cultivation techniques, produced new genetic strains with higher biotic potentials, developed efficient pesticides, and micro-organisms which have a greater nitrogen-fixing capacity. The co-operatives have increased in size and the exploitation of peasants in favour of landowners has become a thing of the past. The American idea of creating a rich peasant society was doomed to failure, but has left behind certain benefits such as machinery, which is now being put to good use.

Crop yields are up everywhere and even soya, previously unexploited, is flourishing. Along the tiny networks of canals, boats loaded up with beans, sesame, maize, potatoes, cassava, pumpkins, durians and melons head for the markets at Hatien, Rach Gia, Chau Duc, Sa Dec, Can Tho, My Tho and Vinh Long. Overloaded rickety buses, old trucks, bicycles and three-wheeler diesel contraptions transport the produce north. Huge 5,000-ton ships anchored in the Hau River at Can Tho are loaded to the brim.

Although there is still not much industrialization, the sounds of rice-husking mills, the smell of shrimp-processing factories and the pungent odours of Nuoc Mam establishments fill the air. Large fishing boats are being constructed at Rach Gia, and Rhizophora forests, previously stunted by chemical warfare, are again being used for house, furniture and charcoal manufacture. Even the contaminated areas of the U Minh forest are being tapped for their poisonous snakes, which provide vital medical supplies for the pharmaceutical industry. The bee hunters of Cau Mau are providing plentiful stocks of honey and the Rach Gia fishing enterprise is getting higher fish yields.

The people are mild mannered and amongst the most naturally courteous. The traveller everywhere is greeted with hordes of smiling faces, who eye the foreigner with an alert inquisitiveness. These people are devoutly religious. Christians, Catholics, Buddhists and Cao Dai mingle freely. Isolated pockets of Hoa Hao worshippers are still seen, particularly in border provinces with Kampuchea. Their 'prophet messiah' Huynh Phu is dead, but despite difficulties created by the French, the Hoa Hao University still stands at Long Xuyen. Ever since the end of the Vietnam War the border provinces with Kampuchea have been subjected to armed attacks. Three thousand people were slaughtered in 1977 at Ba Chuc and 130 in 1978 at My Duc. The people remember well the perils of war, but, for the moment, everything is peaceful.

A canal in the Cao Lanh district of Dong Thap province.

Dong Thap Province

Dong Thap province, known as 'The Plain of Reeds', is reached from Tien Giang province via the Bac My Thuan ferry crossing. A newly completed road is the only motor road crossing Dong Thap Muoi linking Hong Ngu on the Kampuchean border to Moc Hoa in Long An province. It is reported that the residents of Hong Ngu were extremely upset at seeing cars and lorries for the first time ever. The plain of reeds is being developed as a major rice- cajeput- and jute-growing area. A war memorial at My Tra village, Cao Lanh district, displays lotus petals, the symbol of the province. Daily life along the very acid fresh-water canals is an unhurried affair. In the past, Thap Muoi farmers used to grow floating rice, which gave extremely poor yields, but since the road has been built they have been encouraged to grow two rice crops a year. Many more materials have become available and tractors are now appearing for the first time in the

(*Left*) One of the smaller waterways in Ben Tre province.   (*Above*) The market at Sa Dec.

province. An interesting crop grown in the province is Tram Gio, a form of cajeput whose leaves yield valuable medicinal oils. The production of large amounts of jute — Bang and Lac plants — has led to the setting up of industries manufacturing bags, mattresses and carpets. During the Vietnam War Dong Thap was a strong guerilla base, the grasslands, swamps, rows of cajeput trees and the vast lotus ponds giving good cover. There was a massive Viet Cong stronghold in Xeo Quyt district.

The Tam Buu temple (*left*) and its present curator (*bottom*).

The Mekong area more than any other in Vietnam has been affected by events in Kampuchea. As early as 1975 the border provinces were subjected to armed attacks by Pol Pot's troops. The delta also received a large influx of hundreds of thousands of Khmer refugees fleeing from the Pol Pot regime. Some are still resident in the border provinces. The worst armed attacks came in 1977–78, when all the villages on the border had to be evacuated. At Ba Chuc village, Triton district, in An Giang province, 3,000 people were massacred by Pol Pot's troops in 1978. The temples in the area of Phi Lai and Tam Buu still have bloodstained walls, a reminder of the massacre. An ossuary has been built at Ba Chuc village to remind people of the Pol Pot killings.

The Ossuary at Ba Chuc.

Chau Thanh District

Chau Thanh district is reached from Can Tho via Highway No. 9 to Long Xuyen, An Giang province. It passes through an area heavily bombed during the border conflict with Kampuchea. The agriculture in the area is mainly rice, peanuts, sweet potato, manioc and sesame. The road from Long Xuyen runs alongside the An Chau canal, over which there are many monkey bridges. The mountains at Bay Nui, seen on the horizon, were Viet Cong strongholds. Irrigation canals can be seen stretching into the distance. Thot Not after Ba Chuc is well known for sugar syrup manufactured from the sugar palms which grow prolifically in the area. The return journey from Chau Duc can be made via Phu Tan, which is Hoa Hao, Huynh Phu So's native village. He founded the Buddhist sect Hoa Hao in 1939. The followers believed that under the guidance of the Messiah, i.e. the prophet Huynh Phu, that they would be able to build a happier society. His mysterious words and strange behaviour brought him the nickname 'The Mad Monk'. After being jailed by the French and released by the Japanese he developed the Hoa Hao sect into a political organization. His 'army' fought for national liberation until his death in the final collapse of the movement, which did not occur until June 1955, when it was overthrown by Diem.

(*Opposite*) One of many monkey bridges over the An Chau canal, in the Chau Thanh district. This one leads to Can Dang village. It feels as precarious as it looks.

(*Below*) An irrigation canal in An Giang province.

If the Mekong Delta is the chief granary of Vietnam, then the lower delta is certainly one of its most productive regions. The trend towards collectivization in co-operatives means that greater yields of rice have been obtained. Farmers are getting better rice production by transplanting the rice seedlings twice for each crop. Double cropping is becoming the norm, and in July-August and December rice threshing machines can be seen around every corner.

This has created better living standards, more and more peasants are extending their properties and the limestone quarries are in full swing. The production collectives can now buy materials on credit from the state, payment being made after the harvest.

Can Tho is the largest city on the Delta, some 300,000 of the 2.5 million in Hau Giang province live there. The produce of the Mekong—rice, maize, beans, peas, sugar syrup, sesame, potatoes, melons, pumpkins, eggplants, cabbages, fish, wood, birds, frogs, snakes, turtles, medicinal products, etc.—can all be shipped out from here. The university at Can Tho has one of the biggest Agronomy departments in Vietnam, and specializes in research on rice. Many varieties grow in the Mekong granary; they include Lua Tau, Lua Mong, Lua Mo Cai, Lua Can Dong, Lua Chang Co and glutinous varieties such as Nep Den, a black variety, Nep Huong, and Nep Sap. Along the road from Can Tho to Rach Gia, Lua Tau, one of the best varieties in terms of taste and flavour, is threshed by quite modern machines which scatter dust into the air.

(Above) Transporting limestone on the canal from Ha Tien to Rach Gia.

(Right) Water pots being taken to Go Quao — another use for the ubiquitous bicycle.

(Opposite) Rice-threshing machines are round every corner in the Mekong. This one is near Go Quao.

Morning market on the banks of the Kien River at Rach Gia.

Processing plants have been set up all over the Mekong area to deal with the massive amount of produce. The pineapple-processing factory in the Tra Noc Industrial Complex in Can Tho has an all-female staff. They cut, clean, peel, chop, weigh and sterilize the pineapples before they are frozen at $-25°C$. As in the Nha May shrimp factory in Xuat Khau-Rach Gia a high standard of hygiene is maintained throughout the process. The staff here were trained by Norwegian experts. As well as being brought in by fishermen, shrimps are obtained from the shrimp-breeding stations at An Minh and An Bien.

(*Above*) Workers at the pineapple processing factory on the Tra Noc industrial estate at Can Tho. The pineapples are grown at Long My, which is also in Hau Giang province.

(*Left*) The Nha May shrimp processing factory.

Fishing boat on a canal near Hon Dat.

The Xi Nghiep Dong Tau Shipyard at Rach Gia builds boats from 7 to 150 tons. The yard is now government-run, like the fishing fleet which it builds, as part of the Phu Quoc, Fishing Enterprise. Many thousands of 'boat people' found quite a different use for craft like these in the years following the withdrawal of American troops.

The Soc Soai Temple (*above*) and its main altar (*top, opposite*).

The Khmer temple known as Soc Soai is in Hon Dat district, Kien Giang province. The Hon Dat novel is based on a true story about this area. This was written by Anh Duc in 1963. At that time a few dozen guerillas helped by the local people, and using Hon Dat mountain caves as their base, defeated a major force of the puppet regime and its US advisers. The novel tells the story of the fighting which took place and the hardships they endured. It was the first novel about the anti-US war by a Vietnamese writer. Many of the characters in the novel still live in Hon Dat. This includes Ca My, a Khmer girl who now works at the Kien Giang Sea Products Service.

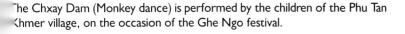
The Chxay Dam (Monkey dance) is performed by the children of the Phu Tan Khmer village, on the occasion of the Ghe Ngo festival.

The Khmer minority are found in the provinces of Kien Giang, Cuu Long, An Giang and Minh Hai. Living in Phum Soc (hamlets), they now number 750,000. Many families have been living on the Mekong Delta for 300 years and still retain their traditions. Towards the Kampuchean border at Triton district in An Giang province many refugees who had run from Pol Pot have taken up residence.

(*Opposite*) The old lady's offerings of rice porridge, a pig's head and wine are for the benefit of passers-by. She is giving thanks to Buddha for the recovery of her son from a severe illness.

The mass grave at Thach Dong about 3 km from Ha Tien reminds visitors of the Pol Pot massacre of 130 people on 14 March 1978 at My Duc. A temple inside a small mountain can be reached from the grave. The temple Bach Van is dedicated to the Buddha Sakya Mouni and the Boddhisatra Quan Am — the Goddess of Mercy. At midday sunlight leaks through a hole in the top of the cave. The temple Bach Van was built in the 18th century and refurbished twice. The first time was during Ming Manh's reign and the second was in 1950. A legend states that Thach Sanh, a wood-cutter, once went past the cave and heard a cry for help from inside. He saw a fierce eagle who had stolen princess Huyen Nga, daughter of Thuy Te, saved her from being ripped to pieces, and later fell in love with her.

The other temple in the area is in Bing An village, reached by road via the Nga Ba Hon bridge. It is situated about 40 km from Ha Tien in an area inhabited by many Khmer people, who live by growing sugar palms. The temple known as Chua Hang (Hai Son Tu) has only 1 monk and 3 nuns in residence. It was built in the late 17th century and contains a most peculiar statue of Sakya Mouni.

(*Right, opposite*) The shrine to Sakya Mouni in the Temple of Chua Hang.

(*Above*) Salt being collected at Duong Hoa, about 20 kilometres from Ha Tien.

(*Top, opposite*) The mass grave at Thach Dong.

(*Bottom Left, opposite*) The shrine of the Bach Van Temple at Thach Dong.